Hawks

Birds of Prey of Minnesota

FIELD GUIDE

by Stan Tekiela

Adventure Publications, Inc.
Cambridge, Minnesota

To my wife Katherine and daughter Abigail
with all my love

Acknowledgments:

Dedicated to Dudley Edmondson, Brian K. Wheeler and Jim Zipp, three outstanding raptor experts and wildlife photographers.

Many thanks to the following people and organizations for allowing their birds of prey to be photographed for this book: Linda and Bill Jansen, Lake Superior Zoo, University of Minnesota Raptor Center, Wildlife Science Center and Wolf Ridge Environment Learning Center. Special thanks to Anthony Hertzel for the range maps, and Dudley Edmondson and Steve Millard for reviewing them. Special thanks also to Sandy Livoti for her exceptional eye to detail.

Book design and nest illustrations by Jonathan Norberg

Bird illustrations and silhouettes by Dudley Edmondson

Photo credits by photographer and page number:

Cover photo: Red-tailed Hawk by Dudley Edmondson
Rick and Nora Bowers: 58 **Dudley Edmondson**: xi (both), xii (both), 2 (perching, soaring, soaring juvenile), 4 (perching, soaring, soaring juvenile), 6 (soaring juvenile), 10 (soaring, soaring juvenile), 12 (perching, soaring), 14 (juvenile light and dark morphs), 16 (soaring juvenile), 18 (juvenile), 20 (soaring male and female), 22 (soaring), 24 (perching, soaring, soaring juvenile), 28 (male, female, in flight), 30 (female, in flight), 34 (female, in flight), 36 (perching, juvenile), 42 (soaring), 44, 46 (gray morph), 50, 64 (both) **Brian E. Small**: 26 (perching) **Stan Tekiela**: 2 (juvenile), 10 (male, female, juvenile), 12 (soaring juvenile), 14 (perching light morph), 16 (perching, soaring), 18 (soaring, soaring juvenile), 22 (perching), 24 (juvenile), 26 (soaring, soaring juvenile, juvenile), 32 (Prairie), 36 (both), 48, 52, 56, 60, 62, 66 **Brian K. Wheeler**: 4 (juvenile), 6 (perching, soaring), 8 (soaring), 12 (juvenile), 14 (perching dark morph, soaring light and dark morphs, soaring juvenile light and dark morphs), 16 (juvenile), 18 (soaring), 20 (perching male and female, juvenile), 24 (juvenile), 26 (juvenile), 28 (in flight juvenile, juvenile), 34 (in flight juvenile, juvenile), 38 (all), 40 (both), 42 (perching, juvenile) **Jim Zipp**: 6 (juvenile), 8 (perching, soaring juvenile, juvenile), 20 (soaring juvenile), 30 (male), 46 (red morph), 54

To the best of the publisher's knowledge, all photos were of live birds. Some were photographed in a controlled condition.

TABLE OF CONTENTS

Introduction

Quick-Compare Pages

Sample Page

The Birds

Helpful Resources

Check List/Index

About the Author

MINNESOTA'S AMAZING BIRDS OF PREY!

Birds of prey are a wonderful group of birds that have captured the imagination of many people. Also called raptors, they include hawks, eagles, falcons, kites, vultures and owls. Hawks, the most common raptors, are seen deep in woods, hunting along edges of forests or in open fields and prairies across Minnesota. Eagles are among the largest and most majestic raptors in the state. Falcons are the fastest fliers, and kites are airborne acrobats. While most birds of prey are efficient predators, vultures scavenge for their food, rarely killing anything. Owls are masters of the dark. Despite the diversity of the group, these raptors have much in common.

Many raptors are large and powerful with unsurpassed abilities to capture prey. A large curved bill allows raptors to tear flesh and crush bone. Exceptionally strong feet, and toes tipped with long dagger-like nails are perfect for capturing and killing small animals. Raptors usually have relatively large eyes and better vision than our own. Eagles, for example, can see much greater distances, and owls can see better in low light environments. Most birds of prey have keen hearing—twice that of humans. Many predatory birds are also masters of the sky, and people are fascinated by their flight. With a single flap, they glide upward on outstretched wings to dizzying heights, or fly in near total darkness. These extraordinary physical abilities set raptors apart from all other species of birds. It's no wonder we stand in awe of these magnificent creatures.

To help you enjoy these birds, the *Birds of Prey of Minnesota Field Guide* has been designed as a handy pocket guide for quickly and easily identifying predatory birds of Minnesota. All hawks, eagles, falcons, kites, vultures and owls that can be found in the Viking State—33 species in all—are included in this full-color photographic guide. Some of the raptors are more common than others; only a few are considered rare.

TIPS FOR IDENTIFYING BIRDS OF PREY

Identifying raptors isn't as difficult as it may seem. Follow a few basic strategies, and you'll increase your chances of successfully identifying most birds of prey you see!

One of the first and easiest things to do when you see a new bird of prey is to note its overall shape. You won't always get a good look at a raptor, but noting the shape of its head, wing, tail or body may be all you need to identify it. Black silhouettes of each raptor are provided on quick-compare and description pages to help you confirm your identification. Silhouettes of how each day-flying bird of prey looks from a head-on flight position will help you to identify it from another perspective.

In Flight

Noting the flight habits of an unknown bird of prey can help you identify it. You may not recognize all of the flight characteristics or patterns immediately, but with practice you'll greatly increase your ability to identify birds of prey when they are in flight.

Hawks are divided into two groups—buteo and accipiter. Buteos are medium to large hawks with heavy bodies, short tails and relatively long, wide wings. These birds tend to fly by flapping slowly and heavily for a few strokes, usually in a series of three to six beats, then gliding on outstretched wings into a series of tight circles until they gain enough altitude to soar. Buteos in Minnesota include Broad-winged, Red-shouldered, Swainson's, Red-tailed, Rough-legged and Ferruginous Hawks.

Accipiters are small to medium woodland hawks with slender bodies, long narrow tails and short, stubby, rounded wings. Their compact design allows them to maneuver between trees while pursuing small birds. They fly in a very characteristic flap-flap-flap-glide pattern consisting of a short quick burst of flutter-like wing beats followed by a short glide. Minnesota's accipiter species are the Sharp-shinned and Cooper's Hawks, and Northern Goshawk.

The harrier is also a hawk, but it is not a buteo or an accipiter. It is the easiest raptor to identify by the flight pattern. Harriers have an extremely low, roller-coaster-like flight that follows every contour of land and vegetation. Wings are slightly raised in a V when gliding, and wing beats are smooth and full. Interspersed in this highly characteristic flight are sudden drops to the ground to pounce on prey. There is only one species of harrier in North America, the Northern Harrier.

Eagles usually fly holding their long, broad, round-tipped wings directly out from their sides. These birds are not fast fliers, but flap deeply and powerfully. Eagles often soar with outstretched wings, not flapping for extended distances, rarely teetering from side to side like vultures. Two types of eagles in the northland are Bald and Golden Eagles.

Ospreys do less gliding and flap more often than Bald Eagles. They have narrow angled wings unlike the wings of eagles. Their bodies and heads seem to bob up and down with each pump of the wings. These raptors fly with almost stiff wing beats that seem to originate near the wrist, not at the shoulder like the other birds of prey. There is only one species of Osprey.

Falcons are in general some of the smallest, but fastest birds of prey. Quick, agile fliers with long tapered wings, they are often seen actively flapping in a direct flight pattern or hovering (turning into wind and quickly flapping), gliding only when absolutely necessary. These birds are well known for their ability to change direction quickly and achieve incredibly fast speeds when diving on prey or during courtship. Unlike the accipiters, falcons have pointed wings. Falcon species in Minnesota include American Kestrels, Merlins, Prairie and Peregrine Falcons, and Gyrfalcons.

Kites are slim-bodied birds with long falcon-like wings and long tails. They have a unique bouncy flight, frequently described as buoyant. They change directions quickly, flying up and down as they chase after insects in midair. Active fliers, they don't spend much time gliding. Wing beats are often slow and can seem stiff. Mississippi and Swallow-tailed Kites are rare in Minnesota.

Vultures fly on long, broad, round-tipped wings, holding them above the level of their bodies in a slight V shape. Their flight pattern consists mainly of gliding interspersed with a few shallow wing beats. During a glide, they frequently teeter back and forth from wing tip to wing tip. We have only one resident vulture in Minnesota, the Turkey Vulture.

Perching

Identifying a raptor that is perched on a tree branch, power pole or other object may be easier than trying to identify one that is flying. Unlike birds in flight, which often fly out of view quickly, perching birds allow you more time to observe them. In general, birds of prey will usually perch upright on branches or poles. This is unlike other large birds such as crows and ravens or even smaller songbirds, which lean out over their feet and approach a more horizontal position.

Buteo hawks are easy to identify when perched because of their relatively small heads, large broad bodies and short tails. They are frequently seen out in the open, along roads or in fields and prairies, making them easy to spot.

Smaller accipiters will rarely perch out in the open. Instead, these woodland hawks perch on tree branches for short periods, then fly off to other temporary perches in search of prey. They have smaller heads, narrower bodies and longer tails than buteos.

Harriers usually perch on the ground and occasionally on low posts. They have small heads, slender bodies and long narrow tails. Look for unusual owl-like facial disks to help identify this hawk when it is stationary.

Eagles are enormous birds of prey that perch bolt upright, often lowering their bodies over their legs and feet. They tend to look like the trunk of a tree when perching because they are so wide-bodied and dark.

Ospreys appear eagle-like when perching, but they are smaller than eagles, with smaller heads and less impressive bills. Their long wings project well beyond their tails when perching. To differentiate an Osprey from an adult Bald Eagle, look for its white chest and belly.

A perched falcon has a compact, flat-topped head and long tail, and appears wider in the middle. Falcons often have a bold dark facial mark called a mustache that helps identify them while they perch. These birds tend to lean farther out over their feet (more like a songbird) than other birds of prey. Watch for some falcon species to pump their tails up and down directly after landing.

Kites perch upright with their long wings and tail projecting well beyond what you'd expect to see in a perching hawk. The round heads and long necks of kites will be obvious when they perch. Because these birds hunt while in flight, you will be more likely to see them flying to and from perches, chasing flying insects.

Turkey Vultures are not often seen perching. When they perch, they often hold their wings outstretched to sun themselves or dry out after a rainstorm. While this characteristic makes these birds easy to identify when stationary, you are more likely to see them flying. Look for their deep red heads and dark bodies to help identify them.

Owls seen during the day usually will be perching, which often allows you to get a good look. These birds are easy to identify because they sit upright on branches, often with legs hidden in the belly feathers. Owls are easier to identify than other raptors because they have large round heads with large eyes positioned in the front of their heads, thick compact bodies and short tails.

WHAT MAKES A BIRD OF PREY?

All predatory birds share some similar characteristics. They have a relatively large, sharp hooked bill to dispatch prey with a deep bite to the back of the neck at the base of the skull, which severs the spinal cord. After the kill, the beak is used to cut and tear flesh and crush bones of the prey.

The size of a raptor's bill is in direct proportion to what it hunts and eats. Eagles eat a wide variety of prey and require a thicker, heavier bill. Ospreys are similar to eagles in size, but feed mainly on fish and thus have a much smaller bill that is appropriate for consuming soft-bodied fish. American Kestrels feed mainly on grasshoppers and other large insects, and have a bill more in line with pulling insects apart.

With the exception of vultures, predatory birds have powerful feet, long toes and exceptionally sharp, long nails called talons. Feet and toes are used to grasp and hold prey. Some birds can actually kill just with the feet. Eagles can do this, some exerting up to 500 pounds (225 kg) of pressure per square inch. Because feet are usually used to capture and hold prey, the importance of a raptor's foot cannot be overstated.

Powerful eyesight is probably the single most important feature of most birds of prey. Nearly all raptors hunt by using their eyes. Any damage to the eyes usually results in the demise of the bird. Eyes of raptors are large in proportion to their heads, and fixed in their sockets. Larger eyes increase the vision power, but force a raptor to turn its head to look around. Owls, which have eyes positioned in the front of their faces, can see up to 100 times better than humans in a low light situation. Hawks, eagles and other raptors, which have eyes positioned more on the sides of their heads, can see at least ten times better than humans in daylight conditions. All raptors have two sets of eyelids. The outer eyelid is similar to a human eyelid, and functions in nearly the same way in most birds. A thin, usually translucent inner eyelid called the nictitating membrane cleans and moistens the cornea. Some believe that the membrane remains over the eye during flight for protection.

Besides keen eyesight, some raptors have outstanding hearing. Owls are known for hunting by sound. Their ears are hidden under feathers on the face, near the eyes. Great Horned Owls can hear a mouse under as much as a foot of snow. It is said that if an owl is near enough to see you, it can probably hear your heart beating in your chest.

Most predatory birds are not brightly colored. Nearly all raptors are light or dark brown, black and white, grayish blue or some combination. These earthy colors help them blend in with their environments. One of the exceptions is the male American Kestrel, a rusty falcon with shades of steel blue.

BIRD OF PREY ANATOMY

Males look identical to females in most raptor species. However, in many species females tend to be slightly or noticeably larger. Throughout the text, the words "slightly" or "noticeably" are used to describe size differences between sexes. When females are only 1 to 2 inches (2.5 to 5 cm) larger, "slightly" larger is used. Females at least 3 inches (7.5 cm) larger are referred to as "noticeably" larger. It is thought that egg laying, incubation and protection of eggs or young while still in the nest are reasons for this size discrepancy, but it is not completely clear why in many species females are larger than males.

Juvenile raptors frequently don't appear like their parents for the first couple of years. They don't need the fancy plumage of adult birds (such as the white head and tail of the adult Bald Eagle) to impress a mate, so they often have less dramatic plumage. Many predatory birds live long lives and take several years to become mature and sexually active, at which time they obtain adult breeding plumage.

It's easier to identify birds of prey and communicate about them when you know the names of the different parts of a bird. For instance, it's much easier to use the word "scapular" to describe the region on the back near the shoulder of a Red-tailed Hawk than to try to describe it.

Labeled images on the next two pages point out basic parts of a raptor. Because one image cannot show all the parts necessary, there are several examples of common birds of prey with labels. Every attempt has been made to label all parts of a bird with the terminology used in the text; however, not all of the anatomy (terminology) of a raptor has been used in this book.

UNDERSIDE (VENTRAL)

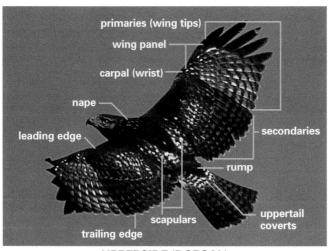

UPPERSIDE (DORSAL)

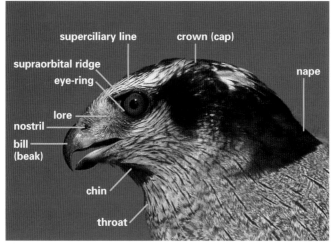

FACIAL MARKING

FACIAL MARKING

BIRD OF PREY NESTS

Most birds of prey construct platform nests. Several species build a ground nest. Some falcons scratch a shallow depression into dirt called a scrape. A few owl species move into natural cavities or old woodpecker holes. Others simply take over existing nests of different bird species. The following describes the different types of nests used by the raptors in Minnesota.

The **platform nest** is a simple gathering of sticks laid horizontally in a tree fork or on a couple of branches near the tree trunk. It usually has a shallow depression in the center, which is sparsely lined with dry grass or feathers for cushioning eggs and young. Sticks and branches are collected from the local area. Birds of prey will occasionally get material for these nests by flying by a dead tree branch, grabbing it and snapping it off. This behavior is common of Ospreys. The size of the sticks used in a platform nest is directly proportional to the size of the bird constructing it. Don't expect to see a small Sharp-shinned Hawk sitting in a huge platform nest that is larger than the raptor itself. Most of these nests are continually enlarged and rearranged over many years and can be used for two decades or more, depending on the strength of supporting structures. Bald Eagles, for instance, will accumulate so many sticks over the years that some of their nests can be more than 10 feet (3 m) deep and weigh over 2,000 pounds (900 kg).

Usually both mates construct a nest. In spring (sometimes fall) mated pairs reestablish their bonds by bringing more sticks to their nest. Sometimes the nest grows so large that it either falls under its own weight or is blown down in a storm.

A young pair of raptors often doesn't build a nest that is large or strong enough to successfully raise a family. While it may take up to several weeks for a young pair to build a typical stick nest, it could take two or more years of work to construct a well-built nest, and several generations of use to make it just right.

platform nest   ground nest   scrape   cavity nest

Occasionally a pair of young birds will start building a nest, but won't lay eggs. The following year they may return to add more sticks to the original structure and then lay eggs. These birds presumably were not mature enough to reproduce the first time they tried. It is not uncommon for a pair of raptors to start constructing a nest, then move to another location and build a second one. This behavior is not clearly understood.

Nests of Northern Harriers are different. This species uses a very simple type of **ground nest**, building it on the ground, or low in shrubs or small trees. Using sticks sparingly, harriers construct their nests with loose grass and other plant material.

A simple nest, called a **scrape**, is a shallow depression scratched into the earth. Used by some falcons, it is usually located on a ledge of a cliff face. It ordinarily will not contain nesting material to cushion eggs or comfort the young. This is the nest of choice for birds such as Peregrine and Prairie Falcons.

Most of the owls won't construct nests. Great Horned Owls, for example, simply take over existing nests of crows, herons and hawks. These owls start nesting early in the year and sometimes are finished raising their young by the time the original owners are ready to move back in. Other owls such as Eastern Screech-Owls and Barred Owls use a **cavity nest**, moving into former woodpecker holes or natural cavities to raise their young. They don't bring in any nesting material, but simply lay eggs on the cavity floor. Some people have had luck attracting these birds to their properties by installing wooden nest boxes, which mimic natural cavities.

Fledging

The interval of time after a bird hatches until it learns to fly or leaves the nest is known as fledging. Baby raptors are altricial (which means they hatch blind and nearly featherless), and remain in the nest for up to two months. During this time, their eyes mature, flight muscles build and feathers develop. Even after the wings are strong enough to allow young birds of prey to leave the nest, they have much to learn about flight and hunting before they can be self-sufficient.

Unlike many other birds, the young of several species of raptors will return to their nests or scrapes even after they have learned to fly. Using the nest to roost at night, it is also a convenient place for them to rest and get fed. This behavior is seen in young Ospreys. Most other birds don't use their nests again after fledging. Once those birds leave the nest, they never return.

MIGRATING AND NON-MIGRATING RAPTORS

Most hawks, eagles, falcons, kites and vultures migrate, but some do not. Migration occurs due to a number of complicating factors. One part of this complex puzzle is food. Many raptors migrate to areas with high concentrations of food to ensure that a steady food source, such as insects or small mammals, is available to feed their young.

All migrating raptors are not the same type. **Complete migrators** have predictable movements. They usually leave at set times and go to the same places each year to find available food. Broad-winged Hawks are typical complete migrators. At nearly the same time every year, they migrate to the Central and South American tropics. In spring, they return to take advantage of the ample supply of insects, rodents and snakes here in Minnesota.

Complete migrators may travel incredible distances, sometimes as much as 15,000 miles (24,150 km) or more in a year, but birds that move only a few hundred miles or just far enough south to escape winter are also complete migrators.

There are other interesting aspects to complete migrators. In the spring, males often migrate a few weeks before females, arriving back at their nesting sites to defend their territories. In many species, females and their young leave early in the fall, usually two to four weeks before the adult males.

The best place in Minnesota to witness this natural spectacle of migration is at the Hawk Ridge Nature Reserve in Duluth. Each autumn, tens of thousands of migrating Broad-winged Hawks and other birds of prey pass over the ridge on their way south.

Raptors that usually wait until food supplies dwindle before they are forced to fly south are **partial migrators**. Unlike complete migrators, which have set migration times and patterns, partial migrators such as American Kestrels will move only far enough south or occasionally east and west to find abundant food. In some years, the distance may be only a few hundred miles, while in other years it might be nearly a thousand. American Kestrels and Red-tailed Hawks frequently move into towns and cities where they find enough to eat along busy highways or in backyards. This kind of partial migration, dependent upon weather and available food, is sometimes called **seasonal movement**.

Unlike the predictable ebbing and flowing behavior of complete migrators or seasonal movement of partial migrators, **irruptive migrators** move unpredictably or only every third to fifth year or, in some cases, every tenth year. Irruptive migrations are triggered when times are very tough and food is scarce, or the population density of a species is too high. The Snowy Owl and Northern Goshawk are good examples of irruptive migrators. We can see them in some winters in great numbers, while in other winters they are absent.

Migrating hawks, eagles, falcons, kites and vultures are daytime flying raptors that generally rest at night. They hunt early in the morning and begin migrating when soaring conditions are good, after the sun warms up the land. Migrators use a combination of landforms, rivers, and the rising and setting sun to guide them in the right direction. Slowly making their way south or north, they glide on rising columns of warm air (thermals), which hold them aloft. Wind also plays a big part. In autumn, migrators are helped by tail winds from the north or northwest. These winds push birds along, enabling them to exert less energy than when fighting headwinds. Wind is equally important in the spring, since more predatory birds return when winds from the south are strong.

Non-migrators do not fly far from their home territory. Usually sedentary birds, non-migrators such as Great Horned Owls and Eastern Screech-Owls will remain in the same area all year long. Ornithologists are just now learning that some raptor varieties previously thought to be complete migrators are actually non-migrators. This is the case with Peregrine Falcons. For reasons that are not well understood, some races (subspecies) of this species migrate, while others do not.

HOW TO USE THIS GUIDE

This field guide was designed to be taken with you to help you identify raptors that you see flying or perching. The color photographs and accurate illustrations are ideal for anyone trying to learn more about birds of prey of Minnesota.

To help you quickly and easily identify birds of prey, this book is organized by species of birds. The hawks are first, followed by eagles, falcons, kites, the vulture and owls. Individual sections are arranged by size beginning with the smaller birds. Sections may also incorporate the average size in a range, which reflects size differences between male and female birds.

Special quick-compare pages, beginning on page xx, are useful for studying shapes, postures and colors of raptors before heading out into the field. These pages are a great place to start the identification process and make overall comparisons among the birds. For quick and easy reference, the illustrations, silhouettes and photographs are labeled with common names of the raptors and page numbers. Simply make comparisons with the bird you see. For detailed information and to confirm its identity, refer to the description pages.

Many people first see a raptor while it is in flight. Since birds of prey frequently show a characteristic shape and noticeable field marks when they fly, the first section of quick-compare pages shows illustrations of all the day-flying raptors as they would appear in flight. Because you're more likely to see owls perching, illustrations of the 12 owls as they would appear perching are also included.

The second section of quick-compare pages shows silhouettes of wing postures and in-flight views of the 21 day-flying raptors.

The third section of quick-compare pages contains photographs of the 21 day-flying raptors, showing what the birds actually look like while they are in flight.

Photographs of all 33 raptors while they are perching are included in the fourth and final section of quick-compare pages.

Since there are only 33 species of predatory birds in this field guide, just paging through the sections is another good way to determine the identity of a bird in question. If you already know the name of the bird, check the index for the page number.

Range Maps

Individual range maps are included for each bird. Colored areas indicate where in Minnesota a particular predatory bird is most likely to be found. Green is used for summer, blue for winter, red for year-round and yellow for areas where the bird of prey is seen during migration. Purple dots are used for raptors that aren't very common or are rare and indicate where a species has been reported during the previous 20 years. While every effort has been made to depict these ranges accurately, they are only general guidelines. Ranges actually change on an ongoing basis due to a variety of factors. Changes in weather, abundance of species, landscape, human disturbance, and vital resources such as the availability of food and water can affect local populations, migration and movements, causing birds of prey to be found in areas that are atypical for the species.

Colored areas simply mean bird sightings for that species have been frequent in those areas and less frequent in the others. Please use the maps as intended—as general guides only.

Enjoy the Birds of Prey!

Stan

Illustrations depicting shape and field marks

HAWKS   pg. 3
Sharp-shinned Hawk

HAWKS   pg. 5
Broad-winged Hawk

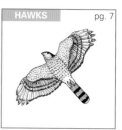
HAWKS   pg. 7
Cooper's Hawk

HAWKS   pg. 9
Red-shouldered Hawk

HAWKS   pg. 11
Swainson's Hawk

HAWKS   pg. 13
Red-tailed Hawk

HAWKS   pg. 15
Rough-legged Hawk

HAWKS   pg. 17
Ferruginous Hawk

HAWKS   pg. 19
Northern Goshawk

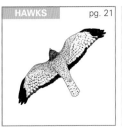

HAWKS pg. 21

Northern Harrier

OSPREY pg. 23

Osprey

EAGLES pg. 25

Bald Eagle

EAGLES pg. 27

Golden Eagle

FALCONS pg. 29

American Kestrel

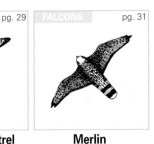

FALCONS pg. 31

Merlin

FALCONS pg. 33

Prairie Falcon

FALCONS pg. 35

Peregrine Falcon

FALCONS pg. 37

Gyrfalcon

KITES   pg. 39

Mississippi Kite

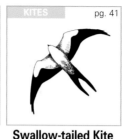

KITES   pg. 41

Swallow-tailed Kite

VULTURE   pg. 43

Turkey Vulture

OWLS   pg. 45

N. Saw-whet Owl

OWLS   pg. 47

Eastern Screech-Owl

OWLS   pg. 49

Burrowing Owl

OWLS   pg. 51

Boreal Owl

OWLS   pg. 53

Long-eared Owl

OWLS   pg. 55

Short-eared Owl

OWLS pg. 57

Northern Hawk Owl

OWLS pg. 59

Barn Owl

OWLS pg. 61

Barred Owl

OWLS pg. 63

Great Horned Owl

OWLS pg. 65

Snowy Owl

OWLS pg. 67

Great Gray Owl

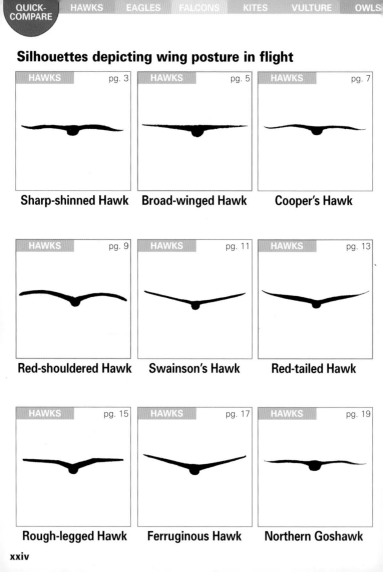

Silhouettes depicting wing posture in flight

pg. 3

Sharp-shinned Hawk

pg. 5

Broad-winged Hawk

pg. 7

Cooper's Hawk

pg. 9

Red-shouldered Hawk

pg. 11

Swainson's Hawk

pg. 13

Red-tailed Hawk

pg. 15

Rough-legged Hawk

pg. 17

Ferruginous Hawk

pg. 19

Northern Goshawk

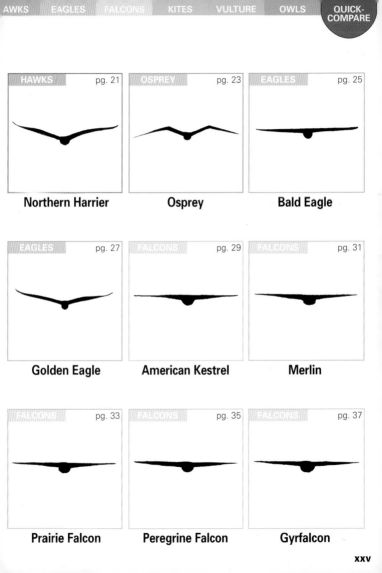

Northern Harrier — pg. 21 (HAWKS)

Osprey — pg. 23 (OSPREY)

Bald Eagle — pg. 25 (EAGLES)

Golden Eagle — pg. 27 (EAGLES)

American Kestrel — pg. 29 (FALCONS)

Merlin — pg. 31 (FALCONS)

Prairie Falcon — pg. 33 (FALCONS)

Peregrine Falcon — pg. 35 (FALCONS)

Gyrfalcon — pg. 37 (FALCONS)

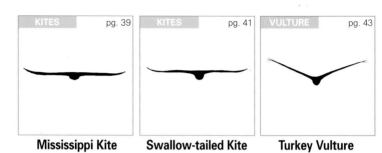

KITES   pg. 39
KITES   pg. 41
VULTURE   pg. 43

Mississippi Kite   **Swallow-tailed Kite**   **Turkey Vulture**

Photographs of raptors in flight

HAWKS   pg. 3

Sharp-shinned Hawk

HAWKS   pg. 5

Broad-winged Hawk

HAWKS   pg. 7

Cooper's Hawk

HAWKS   pg. 9

Red-shouldered Hawk

HAWKS   pg. 11

Swainson's Hawk

HAWKS   pg. 13

Red-tailed Hawk

HAWKS   pg. 15

Rough-legged Hawk

HAWKS   pg. 17

Ferruginous Hawk

HAWKS   pg. 19

Northern Goshawk

Northern Harrier
pg. 21

Osprey
pg. 23

Bald Eagle
pg. 25

Golden Eagle
pg. 27

American Kestrel
pg. 29

Merlin
pg. 31

Prairie Falcon
pg. 33

Peregrine Falcon
pg. 35

Gyrfalcon
pg. 37

KITES   pg. 39

Mississippi Kite

KITES   pg. 41

Swallow-tailed Kite

VULTURE   pg. 43

Turkey Vulture

Photographs of raptors perching

Sharp-shinned Hawk

Broad-winged Hawk

Cooper's Hawk

Red-shouldered Hawk

Swainson's Hawk

Red-tailed Hawk

Rough-legged Hawk

Ferruginous Hawk

Northern Goshawk

HAWKS pg. 21

Northern Harrier

OSPREY pg. 23

Osprey

EAGLES pg. 25

Bald Eagle

EAGLES pg. 27

Golden Eagle

FALCONS pg. 29

American Kestrel

FALCONS pg. 31

Merlin

FALCONS pg. 33

Prairie Falcon

FALCONS pg. 35

Peregrine Falcon

FALCONS pg. 37

Gyrfalcon

KITES pg. 39

Mississippi Kite

KITES pg. 41

Swallow-tailed Kite

VULTURE pg. 43

Turkey Vulture

OWLS pg. 45

N. Saw-whet Owl

OWLS pg. 47

Eastern Screech-Owl

OWLS pg. 49

Burrowing Owl

OWLS pg. 51

Boreal Owl

OWLS pg. 53

Long-eared Owl

OWLS pg. 55

Short-eared Owl

OWLS — pg. 57

Northern Hawk Owl

OWLS — pg. 59

Barn Owl

OWLS — pg. 61

Barred Owl

OWLS — pg. 63

Great Horned Owl

OWLS — pg. 65

Snowy Owl

OWLS — pg. 67

Great Gray Owl

COMMON NAME
Scientific name

SHAPE

YEAR-ROUND
MIGRATION
SUMMER
WINTER
LAST REPORTED

Size: measures head to tail, includes wingspan

Male: brief description of the male

Female: brief description of the female, often indicating a size difference

Juvenile: brief description of the juvenile

Nest: the kind of nest the bird builds to raise its young; who builds the nest; how many broods per year

Eggs: how many eggs you can expect to see in a nest; color and marking

Incubation: the average time parents spend incubating eggs; who does the incubation

Fledging: the average time young spend in the nest after hatching but before they leave the nest; who does the most "childcare" and feeding

Migration: complete (consistent), partial migrator (seasonal, destination varies), irruptive (unpredictable, depends on food supply), non-migrator; additional comments

Food: what the bird eats most of the time (e.g., other birds, mammals, reptiles, amphibians, insects, fish, carrion)

Compare: notes about other birds that look similar, and the pages on which they can be found

Stan's Notes: Interesting gee-whiz natural history information. This could be something to look or listen for, or something to help positively identify the bird. Also includes remarkable features.

soaring

soaring juvenile

juvenile

SHARP-SHINNED HAWK
Accipiter striatus

Size: 10-14" (25-36 cm); up to 2-foot wingspan

Male: Small round head with blue-gray back and head. Rusty red bars on white breast. Long squared-off tail with a few alternating dark and light bands. Red eyes. In flight, head barely projects beyond the bend in wings (wrists), which are usually thrust forward.

Female: same as male, usually noticeably larger, up to one-third larger

Juvenile: same size as adults, heavily streaked breast, brown back, yellow-to-orange eyes

Nest: platform; female builds; 1 brood

Eggs: 4-5; white with brown markings

Incubation: 32-35 days; female incubates

Fledging: 24-27 days; female and male feed young

Migration: complete, to southern states, Mexico and Central America, non-migrator in southern MN

Food: birds, small mammals

Compare: Smaller than the Cooper's Hawk (pg. 7), with a smaller head, square tip of tail (tail feathers are all the same length) and long stick-like legs.

Stan's Notes: A hawk of backyards and woodlands. Swoops in on feeder birds. Short rounded wings and a long tail allow navigation through thick stands of trees to pursue prey. Common name comes from the sharp keel on the leading edge of "shin," actually below the bird's ankle on the tarsus bone of foot. The tarsus in most birds is round. In flight, head doesn't protrude as far as head of Cooper's. Most migrate, but some stay during winter in southern Minnesota.

3

soaring

soaring juvenile

juvenile

BROAD-WINGED HAWK
Buteo platypterus

MIGRATION
SUMMER

Size: 14-19" (36-48 cm); up to 3-foot wingspan

Male: Brown head, back and upperwings. White breast with rusty red horizontal bars. Some have a solid brown breast, forming a bib. A wide dark subterminal band on tail. Short wide wings. Unmarked white underwings with black "fingertips" and narrow band on trailing edge.

Female: same as male

Juvenile: vertical brown streaks on breast and belly, trailing edge of wings has a narrow dusky gray band, numerous narrow tail bands

Nest: platform; female and male build, but the female finishes; 1 brood

Eggs: 2-3; off-white with brown markings

Incubation: 28-32 days; female incubates, male feeds female during incubation

Fledging: 34-35 days; female and male feed young

Migration: complete, to Central and South America

Food: small mammals, birds, insects, snakes, frogs

Compare: Similar size as Red-shouldered Hawk (pg. 9), which shares the rusty breast but lacks the rufous shoulders, and white spots on wings and back.

Stan's Notes: Very common, seen migrating in early fall in large groups (kettles). More abundant than other migrating hawks seen at Hawk Ridge in Duluth. Short round wings propel it as it hunts in dense woods. A high-pitched, whistle-like repetitive "call" if intruders are near nest.

soaring

soaring juvenile

juvenile

COOPER'S HAWK
Accipiter cooperii

Size: 14-20" (36-50 cm); up to 2½-foot wingspan

Male: Bluish-gray head, neck, back, upperwings. White horizontal bars on a rusty red breast. Large squared head. Long rounded tail with several dark bands and wide light band on tip (terminal). Dark red eyes. In flight, head projects well beyond the wrists, which are usually not thrust forward.

Female: similar to male, up to one-third larger

Juvenile: brown head and back with brown streaks on white breast, bright yellow eyes

Nest: platform; male and female build; 1 brood

Eggs: 2-4; greenish with brown markings

Incubation: 32-36 days; female and male incubate

Fledging: 28-32 days; male and female feed young

Migration: partial to complete, to southern states and Mexico, non-migrator in southeastern MN

Food: small birds, mammals

Compare: Larger than Sharp-shinned Hawk (pg. 3), Cooper's has a larger head, shorter stocky legs and rounded-off tail (tail feather length is unequal). Unlike Sharp-shinned, wrists are usually not thrust forward as seen in flight.

Stan's Notes: Like other accipiters, flies with long glides followed by a few quick flaps. In flight, look for its large head, short straight wings and rounded long tail. Known to ambush prey, will fly into heavy brush or run on the ground in pursuit. Nestlings have gray eyes that turn yellow at 1 year of age and dark red when mature.

7

soaring

soaring juvenile

juvenile

RED-SHOULDERED HAWK
Buteo lineatus

MIGRATION
SUMMER

Size: 15-19" (38-48 cm); up to 3½-foot wingspan

Male: Brown head, back and upperwings. Rufous (reddish) chest, shoulders and belly. White spots on the wings and back. Dark rounded tail with thin light bands. Shoulders and rusty red wing linings obvious during flight.

Female: same as male, usually slightly larger

Juvenile: similar to adults, lacks the rusty red color, has a white chest with dark spots

Nest: platform, female and male build; 1 brood

Eggs: 2-4; white with dark markings

Incubation: 27-29 days; female and male incubate

Fledging: 39-45 days; female and male feed young

Migration: partial to complete; winters in the U.S.

Food: reptiles, amphibians, large insects, birds

Compare: Cooper's Hawk (pg. 7) shares the rufous chest and belly, but has a much longer tail. Broad-winged Hawk (pg. 5) lacks the rusty red wing linings (underwing coverts). Red-tailed Hawk (pg. 13) is larger and has a white breast with a brown belly band.

Stan's Notes: Hunts along forest edges, spotting snakes, frogs, an occasional small bird and other prey as it perches. Often seen flapping with an alternating gliding pattern. Very vocal hawk with a distinct, savage-like wild scream. Stays in same territory for many years. Mates when 2 to 3 years old. Starts building nest in February, with young leaving the nest by June. Five races (subspecies) recognized in North America. Not as common as other nesting (resident) buteos.

soaring

male

soaring juvenile

female

juvenile

SWAINSON'S HAWK
Buteo swainsoni

MIGRATION
SUMMER

Size: 21" (53 cm); up to 4½-foot wingspan

Male: Overall brown with a white belly, forehead and chin. Warm rusty breast. Long pointed wings, two-toned with creamy wing linings (underwing coverts) and dark trailing edges.

Female: same as male, but usually larger and tends to be darker and heavily marked

Juvenile: nearly white head, a heavily marked white breast and belly

Nest: platform; female and male build; 1 brood

Eggs: 2-4; bluish or white, some brown markings

Incubation: 28-35 days; female and male incubate

Fledging: 28-30 days; female and male feed young

Migration: complete, to Central and South America

Food: insects, small mammals, snakes, birds

Compare: The Red-tailed Hawk (pg. 13) has a white chest with brown belly band. Look for the Swainson's long candlestick-shaped wings with a two-toned underwing pattern. The underwings of Ferruginous Hawk (pg. 17) are nearly all white with rusty wing linings.

Stan's Notes: Slender open country hawk. Hunts soaring (kiting) or perching. Often soars with slightly upturned wings in a teetering, vulture-like flight. Follows tractors in fields, hunting large insects and displaced rodents. Highly variable in plumage (polymorphic) with three color morphs–light, intermediate and dark. The light morph (shown) is the most common and the one usually seen in Minnesota. Often gathers in large flocks to migrate.

11

soaring

soaring juvenile

juvenile

RED-TAILED HAWK
Buteo jamaicensis

YEAR-ROUND
SUMMER

Size: 19-25" (48-63 cm); up to 4-foot wingspan

Male: Ranges from chocolate brown to nearly all white. Brown head, white chin. Breast often with a distinctive brown belly band but sometimes clear. Rust red tail, usually only seen from above. White underwings with a small dark patch on leading edge near shoulder (patagial). Two nearly white areas forming a V on the back (scapulars) are easy field marks, seen when perched. Brown eyes. Large heavy bill.

Female: same as male, only slightly larger

Juvenile: lacks the red tail, light and dark narrow bands on tail, longer than adult tail, often a speckled chest, dark belly band, light eyes

Nest: platform; male and female build; 1 brood

Eggs: 2-3; white, without markings or sometimes marked with brown

Incubation: 30-35 days; female and male incubate

Fledging: 45-46 days; male and female feed young

Migration: partial migrator to non-migrator

Food: mice, birds, snakes, insects, mammals

Compare: Swainson's Hawk (pg. 11) is slimmer with longer, more pointed two-toned wings and longer tail, and lacks patagial mark.

Stan's Notes: Most common resident hawk, seen perched on freeway light posts, fences and trees. Hunts by perching, circling high above or stalling in wind over fields and roadsides. Large stick nests are used for many years. Doesn't develop red tail until second year.

13

soaring

light morph

soaring juvenile

juvenile

soaring

dark morph

soaring juvenile

juvenile

ROUGH-LEGGED HAWK
Buteo lagopus

MIGRATION
WINTER

Size: 22" (56 cm); up to 4½-foot wingspan

Male: Several plumages. Each has a long tail with a dark subterminal band. Dark band on the trailing edge of relatively long wings. Often a dark belly and axillaries. Feathered legs. Small bill and feet. Light morph is more common, with white under-wings and large dark wrist (carpal) marks. Dark morph has a nearly all-brown body and under-wing coverts, and light gray trailing half of wings.

Female: similar to male, usually larger

Juvenile: similar to adults, lacks a dark band on trailing edge of wings and dark subterminal tail band

Nest: platform, on edge of a cliff; female and male build, or use a hawk or eagle nest; 1 brood

Eggs: 2-6; white without markings

Incubation: 28-31 days; female and male incubate

Fledging: 39-43 days; female and male feed young

Migration: complete, to the northern half of the U.S.

Food: small mammals, birds, snakes, large insects

Compare: Red-tailed Hawk (pg. 13) has a belly band' and lacks the large dark wrist marks. Osprey (pg. 23) has similar dark wrist marks, but lacks the Rough-legged's dark belly.

Stan's Notes: Common in winter. More numerous in some years than others. Smaller, weaker feet than other raptors. Hunts smaller prey, usually hovering before diving for mice or voles. Often feeds on the ground. Nests in Canada's Northwest Territories and Alaska. Perches on surprisingly thin branches.

15

soaring

soaring juvenile

juvenile

FERRUGINOUS HAWK
Buteo regalis

MIGRATION

Size: 23" (58 cm); up to 4½-foot wingspan

Male: Pale brown head, gray cheeks, rufous (reddish) back. White chin, chest and belly. A warm rusty flank extending down feathered legs. Wings have bright white undersides with light rufous linings (underwing coverts). Tail is white below, rufous-tinged on top. Long narrow wings with dark-tipped white primaries. Large, powerful yellow feet. Red eyes and dark eye line.

Female: same as male, noticeably larger

Juvenile: brown head, nape and wings, a white chin, chest and belly, usually lacking any rufous

Nest: platform, low in a tree; occasionally on the ground; female and male build; 1 brood

Eggs: 2-4; bluish or white, can have brown marks

Incubation: 28-33 days; female and male incubate

Fledging: 44-48 days; female and male feed young

Migration: complete, to southern states and Mexico

Food: larger mammals, snakes, insects, birds

Compare: The smaller Swainson's Hawk (pg. 11) has a distinctive two-toned underwing pattern and brown chest. Red-tailed Hawk (pg. 13) has a brown belly band, and lacks the rusty flanks and legs.

Stan's Notes: Our largest buteo, this hawk of western prairies often stands on the ground. Performs an aerial courtship, soaring with wings held above back, male diving at female, grabbing each other with feet. Frequently hunts jack rabbits. Common name means "iron-like." Constructs an extremely large nest. Doesn't nest in Minnesota.

soaring

soaring juvenile

juvenile

YEAR-ROUND
WINTER

NORTHERN GOSHAWK
Accipiter gentilis

Size: 21-26" (53-66 cm); up to 3½-foot wingspan

Male: Black cap. Prominent white eyebrows. Blue-gray back and upperwings. Light gray chest and belly. Gray underwings with fine dark barring. White undertail coverts. Eyes are deep red to mahogany. Yellow feet.

Female: similar to male, noticeably larger, barring on the chest is more coarse

Juvenile: overall streaked brown, irregular dark bands on tail, yellow eyes

Nest: platform, in a tree; male and female build; 1 brood

Eggs: 2-5; bluish-white, sometimes brown marks

Incubation: 36-38 days; female and male incubate

Fledging: 35-42 days; male and female feed young

Migration: non-migrator to irruptive, to northern states

Food: birds, especially grouse, small mammals

Compare: Larger than Cooper's Hawk (pg. 7), which lacks Goshawk's black crown and white eyebrows (superciliaries). Look for Goshawk's gray breast and white undertail coverts.

Stan's Notes: This is the largest of our woodland accipiters. Hunts by chasing or surprising. Highly dependent on the Ruffed Grouse for food, goshawk populations follow grouse populations. Usually seen during migration; juveniles migrate first. Breeds in Alaska, Canada, northern Minnesota and the Rocky Mountains. Usually breeds at 3 years. Female is very aggressive at nest, boldly attacking. The smaller male hunts smaller prey, and feeds incubating female.

soaring

male

soaring

female

soaring juvenile

juvenile

NORTHERN HARRIER
Circus cyaneus

MIGRATION
SUMMER

Size: 24" (60 cm); up to 3½-foot wingspan

Male: Slim, low-flying hawk with dark gray head, silver gray back and upperwings, and white underwings, belly and rump. Faint streaks on the breast and tail. Black wing tips and trailing edge of wings. Noticeable owl-like facial disks. Yellow eyes.

Female: noticeably larger than male, head and back are dark to rusty brown, vertical brown streaks on chest and belly, large white rump patch, thin black bands on tail, yellow eyes

Juvenile: similar to female, with orange breast and no vertical streaks, eyes are dark brown to tan

Nest: ground, sometimes low in a shrub or small tree; female and male build; 1 brood

Eggs: 4-8; bluish white without markings

Incubation: 31-32 days; female incubates

Fledging: 30-35 days; male and female feed young

Migration: complete, to southern states, Mexico and Central America; may winter in MN

Food: mice, snakes, insects, small birds

Compare: The much larger, much darker Turkey Vulture (pg. 43) shares a similar tilting flight pattern, but lacks the Harrier's white rump patch.

Stan's Notes: Characteristic low flight makes this raptor easy to identify. Glides along the contours of the land, holding wings just above body level, tilting in the wind. Will suddenly drop onto prey. Feeds on the ground. Will perch on the ground to preen and rest.

soaring

OSPREY
Pandion haliaetus

OSPREY

Size: 24" (60 cm); up to 5½-foot wingspan

Male: Large eagle-like bird with a white chest and belly, and a nearly black back. White head with a black streak through the eyes. Long wings with black wrist patches. Wings often appear angular or swept back in flight. Dark bill.

Female: similar to male, noticeably larger, often with brown streaking (necklace) on breast, but necklace not reliable for identifying female

Juvenile: similar to adults, light tan breast and wing linings

Nest: platform, often on a wooden platform, tower or in a tall dead tree; female and male build; 1 brood

Eggs: 2-4; white with brown markings

Incubation: 32-42 days; female and male incubate

Fledging: 48-58 days; male and female feed young

Migration: complete, to southern states, Mexico, Central and South America

Food: fish

Compare: Larger Bald Eagle (pg. 25) has an all-white head, tail and large yellow bill. Juvenile Bald Eagle is brown with white speckles. Look for a white belly, dark stripe through eyes and black carpal patches to identify Osprey.

Stan's Notes: A family all its own. Hunts from heights up to 100 feet (30 m), hovers a few seconds, then dives, plunging into water feet first for fish. For better aerodynamics, carries fish headfirst. Often harassed by Bald Eagles for its catch. Lifelong pairs don't migrate to same places.

23

soaring

soaring juvenile

juvenile

BALD EAGLE
Haliaeetus leucocephalus

YEAR-ROUND
MIGRATION
SUMMER

Size: 31-37" (79-94 cm); up to 7-foot wingspan

Male: White head and tail, dark brown body and wings. A large, curved yellow bill and yellow feet.

Female: same as male, only noticeably larger

Juvenile: dark brown with white spots or speckles on body and wings, gray bill, longer tail and wing feathers, appears larger than adults

Nest: massive platform, usually in a tree; female and male build; 1 brood

Eggs: 2; off-white without markings

Incubation: 34-36 days; female and male incubate

Fledging: 75-90 days; female and male feed young

Migration: partial migrator; many will winter along the Mississippi River in southeastern MN, the rest migrate to southeastern states

Food: fish, carrion, birds (mainly ducks)

Compare: The Golden Eagle (pg. 27) and Turkey Vulture (pg. 43) lack a white head and tail. Juvenile Golden Eagle, with white wrist marks and base of tail, is similar to juvenile Bald Eagle. Larger than Osprey (pg. 23), which has a white body and dark wrist (carpal) marks.

Stan's Notes: Minnesota has one of the largest breeding populations in the lower 48 states. Often uses same nest, adding sticks yearly; some weigh up to 1,000 pounds (450 kg). Soars with wings held horizontally. In the midair mating ritual, a bird flips, locks talons with mate, tumbles, breaks away, continues flight. Presumed lifetime mates. Adult plumage at 4 to 5 years.

soaring

soaring juvenile

juvenile

GOLDEN EAGLE
Aquila chrysaetos

EAGLES

Size: 30-40" (76-102 cm); up to 7-foot wingspan

Male: A uniform dark brown body with a golden head and nape of neck. Gray trailing half of underwings, with dark tips. Narrow gray tail bands. Gray bill with a dark tip and yellow around the base (cere). Yellow feet.

Female: similar to male, slightly larger, with an irregular wide gray band across center of tail

Juvenile: similar to adults, often has white wrist patches (variable) and white base of tail

Nest: platform, on ledge of a cliff face, rarely in a tree; female and male build; 1 brood

Eggs: 2; white with brown markings

Incubation: 43-45 days; female and male incubate

Fledging: 66-75 days; female and male feed young

Migration: complete to partial migrator

Food: mammals, birds, reptiles

Compare: Similar to Bald Eagle (pg. 25), lacking the white head and tail. Juvenile Golden Eagle, with its white wrist marks and base of tail, is often confused with juvenile Bald Eagle.

Stan's Notes: Large and powerful, taking larger prey such as jack rabbits. Hunts by perching or soaring and watching for movement. Inhabits mountainous terrain, requiring large territories to provide sufficient food. Thought to mate for life, renewing pair bond late in winter with spectacular high-flying courtship displays. Adds material such as antlers, bones and barbed wire to well-established nest that has been used for generations. Doesn't nest in Minnesota.

in flight

male

in flight juvenile

juvenile

female

AMERICAN KESTREL
Falco sparverius

**YEAR-ROUND
SUMMER**

Size: 10-12" (25-30 cm); up to 2-foot wingspan

Male: Rusty brown cap, back and tail. Dark spots on white breast. White face with two black vertical lines (mustache marks). Blue gray wings. A distinctive wide black subterminal band and white tip (terminal) on rust tail.

Female: similar to male, slightly larger, a rusty cap, brown wings, many thin dark bands on tail

Juvenile: similar to adult of the same sex

Nest: cavity; doesn't build a nest within; 1 brood

Eggs: 4-5; white with brown markings

Incubation: 29-31 days; male and female incubate

Fledging: 30-31 days; female and male feed young

Migration: complete, to southern states, Mexico, Central America, partial migrator to non-migrator in southern two-thirds of MN

Food: insects, small mammals and birds, reptiles

Compare: Male Kestrel is similar to the less common male Merlin (pg. 31), which lacks the black vertical mustache marks. Peregrine Falcon (pg. 35) is larger, has a dark cap and thick mustache mark. Look for two vertical black stripes on face of Kestrel to help identify.

Stan's Notes: Once called Sparrow Hawk due to its small size. A grasshopper eater, could be called Grasshopper Hawk. Hovers near roads, then dives for prey. Pointed swept-back wings, seen in flight. Pumps tail after landing and perches nearly upright. Often nests in a nest box. Unusual raptor in that sexes have quite different markings.

29

in flight

male

Prairie

female

MERLIN
Falco columbarius

Size: 10-12" (25-30 cm); up to 2-foot wingspan

Male: Steel blue back with darker head and tail. A rusty-colored wash to upper breast, sides, wing linings (underwing coverts), undertail coverts and leg feathers. Underwings and breast are heavily streaked. Distinctive wide black subterminal tail band. A very narrow white band on tip of tail (terminal).

Female: similar to male, slightly larger, brown head and back, light superciliary line

Juvenile: similar to adult of the same sex

Nest: platform, or cavity on cliff; relines old crow or hawk nest with feathers; 1 brood

Eggs: 4-5; white with brown markings

Incubation: 28-32 days; male and female incubate

Fledging: 30-35 days; female and male feed young

Migration: complete, to Central and South America; some winter in MN

Food: birds, insects, small mammals and reptiles

Compare: American Kestrel (pg. 29) is similar, but has bold vertical mustache marks. Smaller than the Peregrine Falcon (pg. 35), which has a white face and bold mustache mark.

Stan's Notes: A direct, purposeful flight. Feeds on birds more than insects. In urban areas, nests in conifers and prefers House Finches. Three races—Prairie, Taiga and Black—each appearing a bit different. Narrow pointed wings, dark underwings and a lack of bold facial markings identify it. Also called Blue-backed Jack or Pigeon Hawk.

31

in flight

PRAIRIE FALCON
Falco mexicanus

MIGRATION
WINTER

Size: 16-19" (40-48 cm); up to 3-foot wingspan

Male: Thin bodied with a pale brown head, back and tail. Breast and underwings pale white with small brown spots. Black armpits (axillaries) extending into underwing coverts. Squared head with white area behind eyes. Dark narrow mustache marks. Yellow base of bill (cere), eye-rings and legs.

Female: similar to male, but slightly larger, wing linings (underwing coverts) have heavier spotting

Juvenile: overall darker than adults, heavy vertical streaks beneath, nearly black armpits

Nest: ground (scrape), on cliff face ledge; 1 brood

Eggs: 4-5; white with brown markings

Incubation: 29-33 days; male and female incubate

Fledging: 35-42 days; male and female feed young

Migration: non-migrator; some wander into MN

Food: birds, insects, small mammals and reptiles

Compare: More common Peregrine Falcon (pg. 35) is the same size, but is overall darker with a thicker body and wider mustache mark.

Stan's Notes: A falcon of open prairie habitat (hence its common name) in western states, often wandering out of regular range and showing up in Minnesota. Nests on cliff face ledge, scraping a shallow depression in the dirt. Its unlined nest, called a scrape, always overlooks open habitat. Soars with wings flat. Has the largest eyes in proportion to the head of any falcon. Closely related to the Gyrfalcon.

in flight

in flight juvenile

juvenile

YEAR-ROUND
MIGRATION
SUMMER

PEREGRINE FALCON
Falco peregrinus

FALCONS

Size: 16-20" (40-50 cm); up to 3-foot wingspan

Male: Dark, nearly black head marking appears like a hood. Steel blue back and tail. Breast and under-wings pale white to tan. Belly, legs, underwings and undertail are covered with small dark spots, appearing like horizontal bars. May have a wash of salmon on breast. Wide black mustache mark. Yellow base of bill (cere), eye-rings and legs.

Female: similar to male, noticeably larger

Juvenile: overall darker than adults, heavy vertical streaks on the breast and belly

Nest: ground (scrape), on edge of a cliff; 1 brood

Eggs: 3-4; white, occasionally with brown marks

Incubation: 29-32 days; female and male incubate

Fledging: 35-42 days; male and female feed young

Migration: complete, southern states, Mexico, Central and South America, some non-migrators

Food: birds, Rock Doves (pigeons) in many cities

Compare: Less common Prairie Falcon (pg. 33) is the same size, but lacks the nearly black head and thick mustache mark.

Stan's Notes: The Mississippi River valley and north shore of Lake Superior are the historical range. Due to reintroduction efforts, now also lives and hunts in cities, diving (stooping) on pigeons at speeds up to 160 miles (258 km) per hour. Rural birds feed on many species such as shorebirds and waterfowl. Soars with wings flat. A wide-bodied bird usually identified by its dark head marking (hood), clear chest and mustache.

in flight

juvenile

GYRFALCON
Falco rusticolus

MIGRATION
WINTER

Size: 20-25" (50-63 cm); up to 4-foot wingspan

Male: Largest falcon worldwide. Light gray head, back and tail. Dark horizontal barring on a pale white breast and belly. Back and wings have black horizontal barring. Yellow base of bill (cere), eye-rings and legs.

Female: similar to male, noticeably larger

Juvenile: overall light brown with streaking throughout, has two-toned underwings with paler trailing edge, wider and longer tail than the adults, bluish cere, eye-rings and legs

Nest: platform, on cliff edge; female and male build, or will take over an old nest; 1 brood

Eggs: 3-5; white with brown markings

Incubation: 34-36 days; female and male incubate

Fledging: 49-56 days; male and female feed young

Migration: non-migrator to partial, to northern states

Food: birds (mainly ptarmigan), small mammals

Compare: The smaller Peregrine Falcon (pg. 35) has more pointed, narrower wings and darker underwings. The Prairie Falcon (pg. 33) is smaller, has dark armpits (axillaries) and a narrow mustache, with white behind eyes.

Stan's Notes: Usually a non-migrator, some move south in late fall and winter. Seen only infrequently. Hunts by low flights, capturing prey by surprise. Soars with wings flat. Breeds in Arctic tundra of Canada and Alaska on rock outcroppings. May skip nesting if prey is scarce. Smaller male does most of the hunting during incubation.

soaring

soaring juvenile

juvenile

MISSISSIPPI KITE
Ictinia mississippiensis

LAST REPORTED

Size: 14" (36 cm); up to 2½-foot wingspan

Male: Overall gray bird with a paler, nearly white head and nearly black tail. Dark eye patch surrounding red eyes. Yellow legs and feet. Short, hooked gray bill. Wings have white secondaries, seen in flight from above.

Female: same as male, underside of tail not as dark

Juvenile: brown breast with white horizontal streaks, alternate dark and light bands on the tail, rusty wing linings (underwing coverts) seen during flight, wing tips (primaries) are dark

Nest: platform; female and male build; 1 brood

Eggs: 1-2; white without markings

Incubation: 31-32 days; female and male incubate

Fledging: 32-34 days; female and male feed young

Migration: complete, to South America

Food: insects, lizards, small snakes

Compare: Smaller than many other raptors. The overall gray appearance with a lighter head makes it easy to identify. Rare in Minnesota.

Stan's Notes: A bird of prey that eats mostly large insects. Groups follow livestock, feeding on insects they kick up. Hunts insects by soaring or hovering, catching in flight or diving down. Soars with its wings flat. Requires open areas with scattered trees for nesting. Nests in semi-colonies. Mated pairs aggressively defend nest sites. Doesn't nest in the state. Individuals straying out of their traditional ranges appear in Minnesota.

KITES

soaring

SWALLOW-TAILED KITE
Elanoides forficatus

LAST REPORTED

Size: 23" (58 cm); up to 4-foot wingspan

Male: A white head, breast and belly. Black back, wings and tail. During flight, white underwing coverts, narrow pointed wings, black trailing edge and a long, deeply forked tail. In the right light, the black back and wings appear metallic green-blue.

Female: same as male

Juvenile: similar to adult, with shorter tail, and buffy wash that lasts only a few weeks

Nest: platform; female and male build; 1 brood

Eggs: 2-4; white with dark markings

Incubation: 26-28 days; female and male incubate

Fledging: 36-42 days; female and male feed young

Migration: complete, to Central and South America

Food: insects, snakes, lizards, frogs, mammals

Compare: Osprey (pg. 23) is slightly larger and shares the Kite's black and white pattern. No other bird of prey in Minnesota has such a deeply forked tail.

Stan's Notes: Stunning in flight, the contrasting colors and forked tail easily identify it. Feeds while in flight. Also drinks on the wing, skimming across the surface of water like a swallow. Soars with its wings flat. Rarely hovers like other birds of prey. A very agile flier, will collect sticks for nest like Ospreys, breaking off sticks with its feet as it flies. Semi-social, a couple birds share the same territory. Nested in Minnesota in the 1800s, but quickly decreased. Doesn't nest here now. Individuals stray into the state occasionally.

soaring

juvenile

TURKEY VULTURE
Cathartes aura

MIGRATION
SUMMER

Size: 26-32" (66-80 cm); up to 6-foot wingspan

Male: Dark brown to black with a red head and legs. In flight, wings appear two-toned: dark under-wing coverts with gray trailing edge and tip. Wing tips (primaries) end in finger-like projections. Holding wings in a V pattern, teeters back and forth in flight. Long squared tail. Hooked ivory bill.

Female: same as male

Juvenile: similar to adult, gray to black head and bill

Nest: no nest, or minimal nest on a cliff or in a cave; 1 brood

Eggs: 2; white with brown markings

Incubation: 38-41 days; female and male incubate

Fledging: 66-88 days; female and male feed young

Migration: complete, to southern states, Mexico, Central and South America

Food: carrion; parents regurgitate for young

Compare: Smaller than juvenile Bald Eagle (pg. 25), look for Turkey Vulture's two-toned wings. Flies with wings in a noticeable V shape, unlike the Eagle's straight wing position.

Stan's Notes: Unlike hawks or eagles, has weak feet more suitable for walking than grasping. The naked head reduces feather fouling (picking up diseases and parasites) from carcasses. Developed sense of smell. Urinates on its legs to cool itself. Vomits stomach contents if disturbed at nest site. Mostly mute, it grunts and groans. Seen in trees with wings outstretched to catch sun. Strong bill tears flesh.

43

NORTHERN SAW-WHET OWL
Aegolius acadicus

YEAR-ROUND
WINTER

Size: 8" (20 cm); up to 17-inch wingspan

Male: Small tawny brown owl with wide vertical rusty brown streaks on a white breast and belly. Distinctive light marks on back and wings. Short tail. White streaks on the face, yellow eyes and small dark bill.

Female: same as male

Juvenile: dark brown with a light brown belly

Nest: cavity, former woodpecker cavity; does not add any nesting material; 1 brood

Eggs: 5-6; white without markings

Incubation: 26-28 days; female and male incubate

Fledging: 27-34 days; male and female feed young

Migration: partial migrator to complete, to southern MN and southern states

Food: mice, small birds, insects

Compare: Smaller than the Boreal Owl (pg. 51), which lacks the Northern Saw-whet's rusty brown vertical streaking on chest. Saw-whet lacks the Boreal's black frame around the face.

Stan's Notes: A resident of northern Minnesota, moving in the fall to the southern portion of the state. Our smallest owl, it is not often recognized as an owl because of its diminutive size. Usually found in mixed coniferous-deciduous forests. Strictly a nighttime hunter. Often roosts in cavities, conifers or thick vegetation. Relatively long wings for such a small bird of prey. Common name comes from its rarely heard call, a repeated low raspy whistle reminiscent of a saw blade being sharpened. Can be very tame and approachable.

red morph

gray morph

EASTERN SCREECH-OWL
Otus asio

YEAR-ROUND

Size: 9" (22.5 cm); up to 20-inch wingspan

Male: Small "eared" owl that occurs in one of two permanent color morphs—gray or red. Has dark vertical streaking on breast and belly. The facial disk is outlined with a black line. Bright yellow eyes. Greenish bill.

Female: same as male

Juvenile: lighter than same morph adult, usually no ear tufts

Nest: cavity, former woodpecker cavity; does not add any nesting material; 1 brood

Eggs: 4-5; white without markings

Incubation: 25-26 days; female incubates, male feeds female during incubation

Fledging: 26-27 days; male and female feed young

Migration: non-migrator

Food: large insects, small mammals, birds, snakes

Compare: Only small owl in Minnesota with ear tufts. Can flatten ear tufts and appear like a Northern Saw-whet Owl (pg. 45). Can be gray or rust-colored.

Stan's Notes: A common owl active at dusk and during the night. Will seldom give a screeching call; more commonly gives a tremulous, descending whiny trill, like the sound effect of a scary movie. Male and female give the call, with a slightly higher pitch in the female than the male. Will nest in a wooden nest box. Often seen sunning themselves at nest box holes during the winter. Male and female may roost together at night, and are thought to mate for life. Different colorations are called morphs. The gray morph is more common than the red in most areas.

AST REPORTED

BURROWING OWL
Athene cunicularia

Size: 9½" (24 cm); up to 21-inch wingspan

Male: Brown owl covered with bold white spots, white belly, throat and eyebrows, and very long legs. Yellow eyes.

Female: same as male

Juvenile: same as adult, but brown belly and no spots

Nest: cavity, former underground mammal den; adds some nesting material; 1 brood

Eggs: 6-11; white without markings

Incubation: 21-28 days; female incubates

Fledging: 25-28 days; female and male feed young

Migration: complete, to Mexico and Central America

Food: insects, mammals, lizards, birds

Compare: Short-eared Owl (pg. 55) is larger and lacks the white throat and long legs of Burrowing Owl. Smaller than the Great Horned Owl (pg. 63) and lacks the feather tuft "horns." Spends most time on the ground, compared with the tree-loving Great Horned.

Stan's Notes: Usually the only owl that will perch on short posts or trees, hunting in daytime. An owl of fields, open backyards, golf courses, airports. Nests in small family units or in small colonies. Uses underground dens of mammals, occasionally widening them by kicking dirt backward. Lines its den with cow pies, horse dung, grass, feathers. Often seen in the day, standing or sleeping around den entrance. Male brings food to incubating female, often moving family to a new den when the young are a few weeks old. Will bob its head while doing deep knee bends when agitated or threatened.

BOREAL OWL
Aegolius funereus

YEAR-ROUND
WINTER

Size: 10" (25 cm); up to 21-inch wingspan

Male: Small "non-eared" owl, brown to gray and covered with white spots. Large fluffy head with white facial pattern outlined in black. Bright yellow eyes and dull yellow bill.

Female: same as male

Juvenile: dark gray with prominent white eyebrows

Nest: cavity, former woodpecker cavity; 1 brood

Eggs: 4-6; white without markings

Incubation: 27-28 days; female incubates, male feeds female during incubation

Fledging: 28-33 days; male and female feed young

Migration: non-migrator to irruptive; moves around MN to find food

Food: small mammals, birds

Compare: The Northern Saw-whet Owl (pg. 45) is slightly smaller, more common, and lacks the Boreal Owl's white facial pattern with dark outlining.

Stan's Notes: Usually only seen during irruptive winters, when it hunts for mice along roads or in yards. Often very tame, not responding to the presence of people. Caches food in crevices, tree forks, etc., and will sit on frozen prey to thaw. Many starve to death in the winter when snow cover is several feet deep. Nests in the coniferous forests of northeastern Minnesota. Common name is derived from its nesting habitat. Although not as common as the Eastern Screech-Owl, it is probably more common than thought.

LONG-EARED OWL
Asio otus

YEAR-ROUND
MIGRATION
SUMMER

Size: 15" (38 cm); up to 3-foot wingspan

Male: Overall brown to gray, appearing tall and thin. Thin black line outlines rusty red face. Dark vertical stripe through eyes. Has long black and brown ear tufts appearing close together on top of head. Heavy streaking on chest and belly. Large yellow eyes.

Female: same as male, overall darker

Juvenile: similar to adults, light gray with a dark face

Nest: platform, in tree or on ground; takes over crow, squirrel, heron or hawk nest; 1 brood

Eggs: 4-6; white without markings

Incubation: 26-28 days; female incubates

Fledging: 23-26 days; male and female feed young

Migration: complete, some non-migrators

Food: small mammals, birds

Compare: Smaller and thinner than the Great Horned Owl (pg. 63), with ear tufts close together on top of head. Same size as Short-eared Owl (pg. 55), which lacks the Long-eared's long ear tufts and rusty face (facial disks).

Stan's Notes: An owl of thick, usually coniferous forest. Hunts on the wing at night, cruising over fields and marshes. Male courtship flight is zigzagged with deep, slow wing beats, occasionally with a wing clap that sounds like a wooden stick breaking. Roosts close to a tree trunk during days. Sits erect against trunk for camouflage. Male gives a "hoot" call about every three seconds; female follows with a higher, softer call. May roost with other Long-eareds in winter.

SHORT-EARED OWL
Asio flammeus

MIGRATION
SUMMER
WINTER

Size: 15" (38 cm); up to 3-foot wingspan

Male: Overall brown to gray. Heavy streaking on chest, lighter belly and spotted back. Dark eye patches around bright yellow eyes. Very short, tiny ear tufts are often unnoticeable. Long, slow wing beats. Black wrist (carpal) mark. Large round head. Light face.

Female: same as male, overall darker

Juvenile: similar to adults, light gray with a dark face

Nest: platform, on ground; takes over a crow, squirrel, heron or hawk nest; 1 brood

Eggs: 4-6; white without markings

Incubation: 26-28 days; female incubates

Fledging: 23-26 days; male and female feed young

Migration: complete to partial migrator

Food: small mammals, birds

Compare: Larger than Burrowing Owl (pg. 49), which lacks ear tufts and has a white throat. Same size as Long-eared Owl (pg. 53), which has long ear tufts and a rusty red face. Stiff wing beats and erratic flight make it easy to identify.

Stan's Notes: An owl of northern Canada and all of Alaska, seen mostly during migration and winter when moving south. Like Long-eared Owl, it hunts over open fields, often floating on its long wings just before dropping onto prey. Male calls from high above nest site, soaring, occasionally swooping and clapping wings together below its body. Perches on the ground. Distinctive black wrist mark under wings and a bold tan patch near the upper end of wings (primaries), seen in flight.

NORTHERN HAWK OWL
Surnia ulula

YEAR-ROUND
WINTER

Size: 16" (40 cm); up to 28-inch wingspan

Male: Overall brown to gray. Many fine rusty bars horizontally from breast to tail. White face with a black frame. Dark and light speckled forehead. Broad, flat top of head and bright yellow eyes. Long pointed tail. Small yellow bill. Often covers feet while perching.

Female: same as male, slightly larger

Juvenile: light gray with a dark face, yellow eyes

Nest: cavity or platform; takes over crow or hawk nest, occasionally on top of stump, does not add any nesting material; 1 brood

Eggs: 5-7; white without markings

Incubation: 25-30 days; female incubates

Fledging: 25-35 days; male and female feed young

Migration: non-migrator to irruptive; many move to the northern part of MN in some years for food

Food: mice, other small mammals, birds, insects

Compare: Larger than the Boreal Owl (pg. 51), which has a brown and white chest, and lacks the rusty horizontal barring of the Hawk Owl. Smaller than Barred Owl (pg. 61), which has dark eyes.

Stan's Notes: From northern Canada and Alaska, occasionally nests in northern Minnesota. Often hunts during the day. Uniquely shaped owl, flies like a hawk (hence its common name) with fast, stiff wing beats. Flies close to ground, swooping up to perch on a pole or tree. Can hover. Will use a nest box on a tree. Often unafraid of people.

ST REPORTED

BARN OWL
Tyto alba

Size: 16" (40 cm); up to 3½-foot wingspan

Male: A "non-eared" owl with rusty brown back of head, back, wings and tail. Heart-shaped white face, outlined in darker rusty brown. White chest and belly. Dark eyes. Long gray legs. Gray feet. Yellow bill.

Female: similar to male, often with a rusty wash over the chest and belly

Juvenile: light gray to white, fuzzy-looking overall

Nest: cavity, occasionally on cliff crevice; 1 brood

Eggs: 3-7; white without markings

Incubation: 30-34 days; female incubates, male feeds female during incubation

Fledging: 52-56 days; male and female feed young

Migration: non-migrator

Food: small mammals, birds, snakes

Compare: Rare in Minnesota, easily identified by the white heart-shaped face and dark eyes. The Snowy Owl (pg. 65) is white and lacks the heart-shaped face.

Stan's Notes: Once a permanent resident in southern Minnesota, but now is very rare. Last nested in 1991, 1990 and 1963. Well known for nesting in old barns (hence the common name), but also nests in any dark cavity on cliffs or in trees. Clutch size depends on prey availability–the more prey, the larger the clutch. Young hatch one per day (asynchronously) over two weeks, creating a range of ages in the nest. Will sway back and forth with a lowered head when confronted.

BARRED OWL
Strix varia

YEAR-ROUND

Size: 20-24" (50-60 cm); up to 3½-foot wingspan

Male: A chunky brown and gray owl with a large head and dark brown eyes. Dark horizontal barring on upper chest. Vertical streaks on lower chest and belly. Yellow bill and feet. No ear tuft "horns."

Female: same as male, only slightly larger

Juvenile: light gray with a black face

Nest: cavity; does not add nest material; 1 brood

Eggs: 2-3; white without markings

Incubation: 28-33 days; female incubates

Fledging: 42-44 days; female and male feed young

Migration: non-migrator

Food: mammals, birds, fish, reptiles, amphibians

Compare: Lacks the "horns" of Great Horned Owl (pg. 63) and ear tufts of the tiny Eastern Screech-Owl (pg. 47). Smaller than Great Gray Owl (pg. 67), which has yellow eyes.

Stan's Notes: A very common owl that can often be seen hunting in daytime, perching and watching for mice, small birds and other prey. One of the few owls to take fish out of a lake. Prefers dense deciduous woodland with sparse undergrowth. Can be attracted with a simple nest box with a large opening, attached to a tree. The young stay with their parents for up to four months after fledging. Often sounds like a dog barking just before giving an eight-hoot call that sounds like, "Who-cooks-for-you? Who-cooks-for-you?" The Great Horned Owl sounds like, "Hoo-hoo-hoo-hoooo!"

GREAT HORNED OWL
Bubo virginianus

YEAR-ROUND

Size: 20-25" (50-63 cm); up to 3½-foot wingspan

Male: Robust brown "horned" owl. Bright yellow eyes and V-shaped white throat resembling a necklace. Horizontal barring on the chest. Can be tawny orange around the face.

Female: same as male, only slightly larger

Juvenile: similar to adults, lacking ear tufts

Nest: no nest; takes over a crow, heron or hawk nest, or uses a partial cavity, broken-off tree or stump; 1 brood

Eggs: 2; white without markings

Incubation: 26-30 days; female incubates

Fledging: 30-35 days; male and female feed young

Migration: non-migrator

Food: small to medium mammals, snakes and insects, routinely takes ducks and other birds

Compare: Barred Owl (pg. 61) has dark eyes and no "horns." Larger and more robust than Long-eared Owl (pg. 53). Long-eared has a narrower space between ear tufts. Smaller than the Great Gray Owl (pg. 67), which lacks ear tufts.

Stan's Notes: "Ears" on owls are tufts of feather (horns) and have nothing to do with hearing. Excellent hearing; able to hear a mouse moving beneath a foot of snow. Eyelids close from the top down, like humans. Unable to turn its head all the way around. Ends of wing feathers are ragged, resulting in a silent flight. Fearless, it kills skunks and porcupines. Sometimes called Flying Tiger. One of the earliest nesters in Minnesota, laying eggs in February and March.

male

female

WINTER

SNOWY OWL
Nyctea scandiaca

Size: 23" (58 cm); up to 4-foot wingspan

Male: Pure white with relatively small round head, bright yellow eyes and small dark bill. Feet are completely covered with white feathers.

Female: same as male, but dark bars overall

Juvenile: gray with a white face, then gray changes to white, covered with dark horizontal bars, the younger the bird, the more barring

Nest: ground, often in gravel or atop a hummock; 1 brood

Eggs: 3-4; white without markings

Incubation: 32-34 days; female incubates

Fledging: 14-20 days; male and female feed young

Migration: partial to complete, irruptive; winters in MN, other northern states and Canada

Food: mammals, birds

Compare: Our only white owl, rarely confused with any other bird.

Stan's Notes: A Canada and Alaska nester, known for feeding on lemmings. Moves down throughout Canada and northern states in winter in search of food when lemmings are not plentiful. In some years, may move as far south as northern Texas. The clutch size is dependent on the availability of prey. Prefers to rest on the ground. Male feeds incubating female, but does not incubate. Young hatch several days apart (asynchronously). Families remain together until fall. Often seen on frozen lakes or bays in winter. Blends in with snow. Flies low to the ground on relatively narrow wings with full, stiff wing beats. Shy and unapproachable, unlike many other owls.

65

GREAT GRAY OWL

Strix nebulosa

Size: 27" (69 cm); up to 4-foot wingspan

Male: Overall gray with large, round "puffy" head. Large light gray facial disk with a thin black outline. Black and white throat resembles a bow tie. Yellow eyes.

Female: same as male, only slightly larger

Juvenile: similar to adults, light gray

Nest: platform; takes over a crow, heron or hawk nest, or will use a stump or broken-off tree; 1 brood

Eggs: 2-4; white without markings

Incubation: 28-30 days; female incubates

Fledging: 21-28 days; male and female feed young

Migration: non-migrator to irruptive; moves around MN in winter to find food

Food: small to medium mammals

Compare: Barred Owl (pg. 61) is smaller and has dark eyes. Great Horned Owl (pg. 63) is smaller and has ear tufts.

Stan's Notes: Our largest owl. Nests in northern Minnesota in very low numbers. In some winters, hundreds move into the state in search of food. Detects prey under snow by sound, plunging into snow to capture. Often hunts along roads in winter to capture mice that have left the cover of snow. This leads to many owl-and-car collisions. One of the more active owls during the day. Not often frightened by human presence. During courtship, male gives five to ten deep hoots. Female responds with low whistle or hoot. Some use an artificial nest platform. Young will return to roost in the nest.

HELPFUL RESOURCES:

Birder's Dictionary. Cox, Randall T. Helena, MT: Falcon Press Publishing, 1996.

Birder's Handbook, The: A Field Guide to the Natural History of North American Birds. Ehrlich, Paul R., David S. Dobkin and Darryl Wheye. New York: Simon and Schuster, 1988.

Birds in Minnesota. Janssen, Robert B. Minneapolis: University of Minnesota Press, 1992.

Birds of Forest, Yard, and Thicket. Eastman, John. Mechanicsburg, PA: Stackpole Books, 1997.

Birds of North America. Kaufman, Kenn. New York: Houghton Mifflin, 2000.

Dictionary of American Bird Names, The. Choate, Ernest A. Boston: Harvard Common Press, 1985.

Field Guide to Hawks of North America, A. Clark, William S. and Brian K. Wheeler. Boston: Houghton Mifflin, 2001.

Field Guide to the Birds, A: A Completely New Guide to All the Birds of Eastern and Central North America. Peterson, Roger Tory and Virginia Marie Peterson. Boston: Houghton Mifflin, 1998.

Field Guide to the Birds of North America: Third Edition. Washington, DC: National Geographic Society, 1999.

Guide to Bird Behavior, A: Vol I, II, III. Stokes, Donald and Lillian Stokes. Boston: Little, Brown and Company, 1989.

Hawks in Flight: The Flight Identification of North American Migrant Raptors. Dunne, Peter, David Allen Sibley and Clay Sutton. Boston: Houghton Mifflin, 1989.

How Birds Migrate. Kerlinger, Paul. Mechanicsburg, PA: Stackpole Books, 1995.

How to Spot an Owl. Sutton, Patricia and Clay Sutton. Shelburne, VT: Chapters Publishing, 1999.

Lives of Birds, The: Birds of the World and Their Behavior. Short, Lester L. Collingdale, PA: DIANE Publishing, 2000.

Lives of North American Birds. Kaufman, Kenn. Boston: Houghton Mifflin, 1996.

Living on the Wind: Across the Hemisphere with Migratory Birds. Weidensaul, Scott. New York: North Point Press, 2000.

National Audubon Society: The Sibley Guide to Bird Life and Behavior. Edited by David Allen Sibley, Chris Elphick and John B. Dunning, Jr. New York: Alfred A. Knopf, 2001.

National Audubon Society: The Sibley Guide to Birds. Sibley, David Allen. New York: Alfred A. Knopf, 2000.

Photographic Guide to North American Raptors, A. Wheeler, Brian K. and William S. Clark. New York: Academic Press, 1999.

Raptors, North American Birds of Prey. Snyder, Noel F. R. and Helen Snyder. Stillwater: Voyageur Press, 1997.

Stokes Field Guide to Birds: Eastern Region. Stokes, Donald and Lillian Stokes. Boston: Little, Brown and Company, 1996.

For reporting unusual bird sightings or to hear a recording of where birds have been seen, contact:

Minnesota Statewide	Duluth/North Shore	Northwest Minnesota
800-657-3700	218-525-5952	800-433-1888
763-780-8890		

Web Pages:

The Internet is a valuable place to learn about birds of prey. Following are web sites to assist you in your pursuit of raptors. You may find birding on the net a fun way to learn more about birds or spend a long winter night.

Site	Address
The Raptor Center at the University of Minnesota	www.raptor.cvm.umn.edu
The Minnesota Ornithologists' Union	http://mou.mn.org
Minnesota Birding Network (MNBird)	http://linux.winona.msus.edu/mnbird
American Birding Association	www.americanbirding.org
Cornell Lab of Ornithology	www.birds.cornell.edu
Author Stan Tekiela's home page	www.naturesmart.com

CHECK LIST/INDEX

Use the boxes to check the birds of prey you've seen.

ABOUT THE AUTHOR:

Stan Tekiela is a naturalist, author and wildlife photographer with a Bachelor of Science degree in Natural History from the University of Minnesota. He has been a professional naturalist for over 20 years and is a member of the Minnesota Naturalist Association, the Outdoor Writers Association of America and Canon Professional Services. Stan actively studies and photographs birds throughout the U.S. He received an Excellence in Interpretation award from the National Association for Interpretation, and a regional award for Commitment to Outdoor Education. A columnist and radio personality, his syndicated column appears in more than 20 cities and he can be heard on a number of radio stations. Stan resides in Victoria, Minnesota, with wife Katherine and daughter Abigail. He can be contacted via his web page at www.naturesmart.com.

Other Books by Stan Tekiela:

Birds of Iowa Field Guide
Birds of Minnesota Field Guide
Birds of Wisconsin Field Guide
Trees of Minnesota Field Guide
Wildflowers of Minnesota Field Guide
Nature Smart: A Family Guide to Nature
Start Mushrooming: The Easiest Way to Collect Edible Mushrooms